For those who are ready for my dark.

CCA

Handpicked Roses Volume I

CONTENTS

HELLO   4

Chapter One: THE END   5

Chapter Two: SOMEWHERE IN BETWEEN THE MADNESS   34

Chapter Three: A SERIES OF UNSPOKEN WORDS   52

Chapter Four: A NEW BEGINNING   61

Chapter Five: THE LESSONS   75

CCA

Handpicked Roses Volume I

HELLO

I once heard somewhere that the alternative definition of insanity is the inability to relate to another human being- the inability to love. If you continue reading, you will quickly learn that this book consists of a collection of poems and short stories that tell the journey of a life once lived but never valued,

She had a story to tell but nobody was listening, but that didn't stop her from spilling her mind out on these pages.

As a precaution, there will be no order to this because the chaos of life does not allow for a smooth harmony,

So, stay with me

as I uncover the depths of my own sanity.

CHAPTER ONE

THE END.

She was asked,

"How many times will you let something hurt you?"

She responded,

"Until it breaks me,

Because maybe I'm supposed to let it hurt until it heals"

This part of my story is where it all ends,

And I lose any grip I have on who I am and where I'm
supposed to be.

In this part I struggle to deal with death

my sisters…

my own…

I struggle to see a reason to keep going.

And sometimes I refer to myself in third person, as 'she'
or 'her',

because sometimes I don't feel like me anymore.

~ *thank you for staying.*

Openly broken

I knew something was wrong with me when I woke up

one day and begged God to take me.

Night Terrors…

Held captive by my own body.

Now every time I try to sleep, I get tormented by my

own mind.

She scares me.

I scare me.

The cage within…

I'm hurting inside,

But no body hears me.

I think I like the silence,

The unforgettable darkness

That stands beside me.

Am I alive or am I just breathing?

Maybe someday I'll understand what I'm feeling.

~To be inside of reality...

Writing helps me escape my mind or rather spill my
thoughts into words where they can no longer hurt me.

And for the longest time you were my refuge
Freedom amongst the stars I called it,
because you became my moon.

... is to escape your own insanity~

A letter to self...

I'm sorry I'm not in love with you.

But sometimes I wish to

Not sure of what I feel ...

Not even sure if it's real...

But it feels really intense

Kind of ignoring my sense of self

Maybe if I sit and listen to what she has to say,

All of this pain would go away.

Because I'm having a momentary lapse of insanity

Or perhaps a momentary lapse of honesty

But darling when you are ready,

Please come back to find me,

And save me.

~To be inside of reality...

I have this strange feeling of being tired of being in my
own body
Separate from reality
I kind of want to be out of it for a while
Like just not me for a change
Somebody else
In some place else...
I don't know.

... is to escape your own insanity~

Julio...

I got so used to the dark that I thought grey skies was a normal weather forecast.

~To be a closed book in peace...

I just want to stay in my room forever.
I just want to sink into the pits of my own hole and
simply be forgotten.

...is to master the art of appearing open~

Paralysis part 1…

It all started when I lost her.
Perhaps my brain's way of coping with the pain
Because I feel like I'm going insane.
Sleep paralysis,
It's best described as waking up paralysed with no
control of your body,
where nothing can move but your eyes
When I am under paralysis, I believe I am in the
transition state between real life and the spirit realm
A complete separate plane of existence almost identical
to ours.
So, when I wake up paralysed, it feels so real
When I'm fully conscious, the beings in this realm have
one way of contacting me - the little voice inside my
head,
but they have zero control over me real life.
Sleeping allows them this higher access to me.
It allows them to interact with me and influence my
dream experience.
They can control my dreams but not me or my life.
One thing to note is, I am human, they are not
and they imitate the human anatomy to relate to me and
get closer to me.
But not all of them are friendly,
Not all of them are me.

Paralysis part 2…

> During my paralysis episodes, the embodiment of my
> mind who lives within the spirit realm, comes to me. She
> scares me, I scare me…
> You know that voice inside your head that you think is
> you.
> Everyone's mind exists as a being in the spirit realm, and
> mine came to me in body.
> She looked exactly like me. Everything I thought inside
> my head, she already knew
> because she was and is the embodiment of my mind.

The hidden moon…

There are some days,
where I lay down on my bedroom floor staring at my
ceiling because I have no sky
And there are days I sit in the corner of my prison,
hoping God would someday drop by
Maybe this time He'll come pick me up
Take the right sister instead
Maybe this time, time will reverse and not mess with her
head
There are some days I wake up in the morning wishing I
didn't.
Praying for someone godly enough to come save me
To fix me.

~2 Excuses~1Lie~

I know I'm distant right now

There is no explanation

There is no justification

Maybe I'm just a terrible person

And you are better off

So don't come looking for me in the scarlet forest

Because you might find me amongst the darkness.

~Dear friend if you are still listening...

Sometimes it hurts you know

Because I've never had the direct intention to hurt
anyone

But I have a tendency of pushing away the people that
mean the most to me

I'm not sure why

That's a lie

I am sure

There was once a girl I gave my all to

She was my scarlet in the darkness

After a while she ditched the scarlet part and left me in
darkness

And now whenever I get close to anyone, I have a
tendency of leaving first

Maybe I'm just a terrible person

Or maybe I'm a girl who's decided to guard her heart

And now end up hurting the people I care about in the
process

So, it hurts.

This is not justification, but it is an explanation.

~To be a closed book in peace ...

I've become a master at staying hidden.

...is to master the art of appearing open ~

.

~To be a closed book in peace ...

Anger is the one emotion that I'm so familiar with it
hurts.
Because why am I so angry all the time
I mean everything's alright but
I'm bubbling inside with so much rage
It could eventually kill me.
But maybe that's what I want,
To lose sight of the sky
and eventually dye
my hair red and paint my skin scarlet rose with beautiful
poetry,
Because the right words have always been so pretty.

...is to master the art of appearing open ~

Void…

I haven't been able to cry for the last few weeks.

At first, I thought I was just masking my emotions to
deal with the more important things in my life.

But once I had the time to deal with my feelings, I could
no longer feel them.

Inside is so numb these days

And I need some kind of release, but nothing seems to be
working.

So maybe it's time I pay death its overdue pays.

Slowly losing my grip on reality…

Julio…

I feel like I'm suffocating in my own existence.

Sometimes I try to imagine what it feels like to be

outside of one's mind every once in a while.

Wouldn't that be lovely?

To escape the four corners of this prison built within me.

Everyday feels like a mission to keep breathing, keep

trying, keep living but what for

Who am I fighting to save?

Who am I fighting for?

When breathing doesn't even feel like I'm alive

anymore.

Update...

Update:

She lives in her own dilapidated disturbia

Update:

She is no longer alive.

Update:

With her last breath she whispered

"If only He knew".

Seconds passed,

And her body lay there.

Frozen

Broken

Empty

That's all she left behind.

An empty vessel,

An empty vessel with a smile :)

The outer body experience part 1…

When I was 16, again I went under a state of sleep paralysis, where the body cannot move and only your eyes and mind are awake.

But this time, something was different.

During the time before I had fallen asleep, I was working.

I had fallen asleep at my desk, and awoke to find myself watching myself from behind, still asleep at that very same desk, in the exact same position I had fallen asleep in.

I found myself somehow inside my consciousness yet apart from my body.

Julio…

Sometimes I feel insane.
Like at some point I completely detached myself from
my emotions- from reality
And stopped caring for people the way I used to.
Dear God,

Please help me care again…

Julio…

Hoping one day God would send me someone to talk to,
perhaps calm my mind before I'm taken away by the
depths of my unconsciousness

But I have no one.

And I am starting to accept the fact that maybe that's just
it, I'm not supposed to have someone,

I'm supposed to have me

So, until then I walk alone.

The Birthday wish

I turned eighteen today,

And I feel detached from my own existence

For instance

I mourn the loss of someone once close to me- my mind

She hides

Behind

A smile

Blurred lines between her and reality

I wonder if she'll ever come back to find me

To save me.

I heard that what God breaks, He makes into a masterpiece,

And I'm starting to believe there are some people whose canvasses

never get painted because it's been eighteen years.

When do I stop the breaking and start the making?

Body worn out, my tears dried-I'm tired

Starting to believe the intrusive thoughts that maybe I have

expired.

An empty canvas, an empty vessel

When is it my turn to reach a higher level-

***

***

to be full of love and free of hurt?

Been here a while God, I'm starting to lose my sense of self worth

Can you hear me?

God, are you listening to me?

Why can't you take me?

I'm here

I'm ready

I'm willing

Free me from the shackles of this life

Disconsolation, disconnected

My mind is disconsolate, and I feel so disconnected

Can you hear me, Lord? please take me

Another day, another cry for mercy

please Lord please

I need you to hear me,

to take me,

so, I can finally be free.

My heart was built to love you

I waited for you,
Each night the darkness came knocking in,
I waited for you,
To fight the demons underneath my bed
and not mess with my head.
You were supposed to protect me,
You were supposed to shield me from pain,
Not cause it.
I waited for you,
To show me the love you were supposed to
To be the figure in my life that guided me
Not lead me astray
To teach me where I came from
Not throw me away.
I waited for you because I loved you.
So why did you walk out on me?
Why wasn't I enough?
I waited for you
to hold my hand when I cried

***

***

To bandage my bruise when I fell on the playground.

Instead, you stopped me from experiencing the life I wished

You killed my dreams before I could conjure them

You were the reason I cried myself to sleep

You were the reason I stopped believing in promises

So why do I still wait for you?

To come back

To change

To love me

To be here

But don't worry

You can hurt me all you want

And I will still wait for you

Because my heart was made for loving you.

~To be a closed book in peace ...

Be mindful of the girl that tells you too much,
Her deepest secrets
Because sometimes you think she's opening up to you,
but are you paying attention?
Are you hearing what she is saying?
Is she simply informing you with the context of her
history?
Or is she really opening up to you?
It is so easy to share your trauma without any emotional
tie to it,
I do it all the time,
I am her,
Be mindful of me.

...is to master the art of appearing open~

Julio…

I wish I had someone to talk to
I find myself getting so lost in my own thoughts.
Wouldn't it be nice to share it one day?

But until then
I'll share it with you.
Anyways
Ink to paper has always been quite lovely,
And you have always been quite lovely☺

CHAPTER TWO
SOMEWHERE IN BETWEEN THE MADNESS

Cosmorelated- to be connected by the moon and the
stars.
~ CCA

The light isn't at the end of the tunnel, it seeps through
the cracks in the walls as you walk down it.
It occupies the space it can amongst the darkness,
because even in the mist of sadness,
somewhere awaits your glimpse of happiness.
This chapter is an appreciation of the happy moments,
even if they last just for a minute.

~I appreciate you being here with me, experiencing the
not so bad part,
thank you for staying with me, thank you for not giving
up on me
while I reach a new level in my depth of my own sanity.

Thank you for being You :)

April 27th

> I have a tendency of mourning the people who are still
> here,
> So late at night, when nothing seems right,
> I think of you
> And I remember all the times we shared like it was our
> last
> Four feet behind, I watched you bloom,
> Perfectly imperfect, you became my moon.

The Moon.

You ever sit and wonder what it's like to truly fall in love with someone?

I've lived my entire life till this point not really understanding what the feeling means.

My father taught me that love was pain,

Because the way he loved left bruises

And I used to think to be loved was to be seen,

So as long as he sees me, he didn't need to be nice to me,

Like I was lucky to be noticed,

To be graced by his presence

My father taught me that if you love someone, you hurt them, again and again until they are tired.

And when they get tired, you leave them.

And my mother taught me that love was staying with the one that caused most of your pain,

But then I met him.

And he taught me the way my father loved me was not love,

Because to love someone is to know you have the power to hurt them but never even for a second consider doing so.

***

***

To be loved is not only to be seen but to be heard and to be
appreciated.

And he thought me that I was capable of being loved, and not in
the way my father did.

He also said love was acceptance and I didn't need to filter myself
to be loved,

To be cared for, I could just be me,

And that is why I think I love him.

I...

I want you to experience this love with me.
I don't want to be the only one diving in
Taking the risk to be with you
I need to know you are diving in too,
And we are both starting this journey together.

...was made to love you ~

Us...

Speak to me darling,

Tell me what you want.

Our words create the path for our future

So, create them with me.

Form the life you want us to live

Be with me

In this

And In Us

The Sun

You are a reflection of I

The reason we don't see eye to eye.

Mirror of my soul

Skin like gold

You complete me,

In the worse possible ways

you complete me.

An unfinished jigsaw puzzle,

So come into my arms and be my missing struggle

I miss you,

So, help me see your point of view.

Speak to me

And let us be

Us.

She asked me,

Where does your mind go in between our silent conversations?

     I answered,

     "You"

     "It goes back to you".

     And in that moment, I knew,

     It was you,

     you were the one.

The imaginary friend…

Sometimes, I think I create alternate false versions of reality in my head

I did it when I was younger,

And that's why I seem to have false memories with someone that never truly existed

She was my best friend,

But she only existed inside my head.

How do you get over losing someone who never actually left?

Because she never walked away

She only dissipated,

Because as I grew up, the memory of her simply faded

But I miss her.

She was the first person that shown me what it was like to be loved.

She was the first person that ever truly listened.

Sometimes I think she's back, but it's just her much older and crueller twin, depression.

The skies are always grey with him.

With her, I had no rainy days,

***

***

No lightning storms.

I think as you get older,

Those broken stories you tell yourself to keep your mind safe no longer works,

Because the world becomes too cruel to truly be able to block out

So, as you get older, your best friend,

The one that lives inside your head, goes,

Because she doesn't feel like she can help you anymore.

She doesn't think her light could shine bright enough to cover the darkness of this world.

So, you are left alone,

To deal with your thoughts

And the broken people that claim to love you

but continue to hurt you.

But I think I've met her again,

My blue skies

She came in the embodiment of the most beautiful soul.

And now,

And now he's the half to my whole,

My first love.

~Find your initial in the sign off ~

Sharing my poetry is like sharing a piece of my soul and
I shared it with you,
That's why I can't lose you.
You have seen parts of me people only dream of,
Not that people dream of me, but I mean having the
privilege of truly knowing someone
So now you are my best friend.
So, stay a while
Don't leave me when things get too dark,
Because I will stand by you
Even late at night when nothing seems right.
So dear best friend
I call this one my poem to you
To thank you,
for holding my hand during the dark days.
To thank you for being there even on my distant days
I will always remember you.
And even if we happen to grow apart,
You will always have a place in my heart.

~AIJ~

He was beautiful <3

He was rare.

The sky felt like roses when I was with him.

I will always…

I dreamt about you today.

In the dream, you were hurting so much that I couldn't help you,

I couldn't take your pain away.

I wish I could stop you hurting,

Make it all mine or something.

You once told me how you felt helpless that day,

and even in the depths of unconsciousness

I felt a glimpse of your sadness and I couldn't save you.

I'm sorry,

sometimes I wish it were me,

so, you wouldn't have to feel like someone stole your identity,

but that won't stop me from loving you

Because you will always be my moon.

…be here for you~

I want to be able to write something deep and meaningful like
how the stars aren't the stars and the moon is not the moon when
I'm with you.
And in reality, they are just symbolisms of existence.
I wish I could tell you how the stars exist to show us we are real
and the moon, and oh how the moon exists just for you <3

One day I'll say to him…

I've never been the one to follow the stars, so I'll chase the moon for you ♡

Symphony...

If my screams could sing your symphony,

I would never stop singing for you and me.

Maybe the sounds would pierce the silence

the way your presence

pierced my-

I love you.

Three words felt

But unsaid.

I hate you.

Three words

Unsaid and felt but yet,

I still crave you.

Grey skies and brown eyes

He had beautiful brown eyes.

He set the fire in my heart that only burnt my soul.

Skin like gold,

He had skin like gold.

If time comes for us to separate, just know I love you.

> Not romantically
>
> But platonically
>
> I have the greatest love for you,
>
> And I just wish you had it for me too.

.

CHAPTER THREE
A SERIES OF UNSPOKEN WORDS

Dear *Julio*…

Losing my touch with reality…
losing my hold on me
discovering a new chapter in the depths of my own
sanity.

There is no story or plot to this part. I write down most of the thoughts that comes to my head and now I'm sharing them with you. So, bear with me if they seem random or out of place. The mind is full of chaos and doing this brings me some sort of order, doing this helps me stay together.

"*Sadly, we create the reality we fear due to unresolved past wounds around trust and a persistent fear of rejection.*"- Some article I found online.

*

Psychopath:

The term "**psychopath**" is used to describe someone who is callous, unemotional, and morally depraved.

*

Stop writing about people that hurt you,
Stop writing about people that don't care about you.

~Lalalala I'm blind I can't hear you

*

I think no matter how hard I try, I'll always lose a part of myself trying to love you.

*

There are days where I feel like I'm okay,

        Other days

         I feel like I'm losing my mind and going astray.

I think it's happening again,

> Life's repeating itself
>
> And I'm scared
>
> Because I don't know if I'm strong enough to go through
>
> it twice
>
> It hurt so much the last time,
>
> I'm not sure I'll recover this time.

*

Worst part is I saw it coming, I hurt myself ignoring destiny.

*

I was talking to someone, and I've come to the realisation that I don't have many fears, but the one thing that scares me the most is people leaving.

And I don't know, it's like sometimes I want to maintain a connection so bad that I hold on to the littlest part of it even if it's not healthy.

I'm always afraid people will leave me to the point when I feel someone's energy is off or pattern has changed, I automatically assume it's them wanting to leave.

And I know it's bad, but I can't help it.

My problem is, if I'm not feeling the love, I think it's no longer there.

And I'm just so afraid of losing people, I never even stopped to ask myself,

Are they even afraid of losing me?

There's nothing more ironic than broken people breaking people...

*

Sometimes, I over exaggerate emotions in order to feel validated to feel them.

*

I feel like I'm losing you…

But it's alright, I think I'm starting to accept the fact that you are not here anymore.

*

Sleeping gives her a higher level of access to me and she scares me,

 I scare me.

*

Truth is, I followed the stars but then I lost her,
so now I'm looking for the pieces of myself that once fit perfectly,
to remind myself of who I'm supposed to be.

*

I'd let you break my heart into a million pieces if it meant you were the one putting it back together.

*

She was born out of sadness, so what else do you expect but sad songs and broken poetry.

I don't think music can distract me from this type of pain
anymore...

*

It's okay, you don't always have to label an emotion before you
deal with it

*

You ever feel like some things are just supposed to end?
Like no matter how hard you try, there are some situations that just
aren't supposed to last forever,
and there's nothing you can do but accept it.
people

*

I feel like I'm making the right memories with the wrong people.

*

I'm actually completely fine... just on a different universe to
everyone else sometimes.

*

I'm just tired of being tired and feeling tired,
all the time.

*

Music was my therapy, until it started hurting me
Now I just listen to it to feel something, because sometimes
anything is better than being numb

I just feel like I care too damn much for people who don't even
care if I'm around.

*

So maybe leaving was the only way I could escape the way you
made me feel.
But then I realised,
I caused the pain I was running from,
I was running from my own mind.

*

Spend a lot of my days wondering if I'm ever going to be okay…

*

I don't want to feel any more…

*

I'd rather have a best friend for life than a lover for the season.
I never really liked the temporal nature of people

*

Part of me knows that I'll never find me in another person
But not every part of me is ready to accept that

*

Getting too close to me could be dangerous.

Some people will give you the world and have you thinking

you were supposed to live in it alone…

*

Please, she was never made to experience the love stories, only just

to tell them </3

*

It was never meant to last that long, just accept it for what it was -

temporary.

*

I think

somewhere

 in between

these broken lines

 I found you,

 completely whole.

*

You feel like a summer sunset breeze ♡

*

 Rainbows smell like dead roses when I'm with him

I think deep down, a part of me will always believe that I am a
terrible person.
No matter what anyone says or no matter what I do to prove
otherwise,
I will always be convinced that I'm a terrible person.
And that's why I struggle to believe that there's a single soul out
there that wants to be around me for me
So, I feel guilty opening up because I have this twisted notion that
there is not a single person that actually want to remain friends or
close by, they're just doing it because they feel bad.
So instead, I allow people to open up to me.
Only revealing artificial parts of myself, enough to make them feel
like I'm being as open as they are, but truth is,
I'm ashamed of my truth.

*

You associate anger with love and that is why you love so
violently.

The depths of my own sanity

Before I go, I just have one question for you,
was there any part of you that ever really loved me?

CHAPTER FOUR
A NEW BEGINNING

I gave someone a piece of my soul and they left with it,
so now I'm looking for the pieces of myself that once fit perfectly,
to remind myself of who I'm supposed to be.
-CCA

Que sera, sera…

The consequences for a moment of light

Weather Warning!...

And just like that, you were gone.

The clouds we once admired became our overcast,

Suffocating us to the point where we not only lost each other,

But also, ourselves.

Mastering...

I think I have a tendency of hurting myself,

I start to imagine a world without you.

I think I break my heart sometimes trying to piece our

puzzles together,

but they just never seem to fit.

We never seem to fit.

I never seem to fit,

With you.

...the art of letting go ~

You taught me how to love myself in the ways I couldn't love me.
But even though you've left, I still pray that you are happy.

...Past

I know you'll forget me,

They say the people that care bout you most hear your silence,

So here I am,

screaming silently,

Because I know that you'll forget me.

It was never love that we shared,

It was more of a melody,

It was friendship,

It was everything that we were, and in between,

So, I know that you'll forget me.

The unfamiliar stranger

I think I get it now,

I mean what it feels like

To slowly watch someone you love fade away right
before your eyes,

And there's nothing you can do about it.

I was once told I should allow the people in my life to
come and go as they wished,

Once they've served their purpose, I should simple just
let them go,

Because holding only hurts you more.

Yes but,

No one ever told me how much it would hurt.

And you're right,

I should probably stop sharing my soul to people who
don't know how to handle it,

Because opening yourself up like that to people who
don't care about you any more is only hurting you.

They are only hurting you.

And they will continue to hurt you,

Not because they don't love you,

But because they don't know how to.

Well, I had you,

> And you made my skies so blue.
>
> And I know I'll never tell you this but,
>
> I was afraid to love you.

My fatal attraction

So, this is what unrequited love feels like,

Hiding behind your shadow

Secretly craving you

Secretly loving you

Secretly wanting you.

I never understood what it meant to give someone all of

you so willingly yet so

Secretly

Because my momma told me not to lose my self looking

for kings

but then I found you

And if I told you

Would it be returned?

No?

I didn't think so,

Because this is what unrequited love feels like.

I think I have a tendency of overestimating my importance in
other people's lives

> so, when something doesn't feel right, I step back.

> I thought it was different with you.

> I thought we were on the same page,

> but then you started sounding like everyone else in my
> life.

> You were afraid of my dark, so you left me in it.

> All alone, I stood there, in your shadows hoping one day
> you'd find me.

> But you didn't.

> You walked away and I couldn't.

> Now you're you,

> And I'm me

> Still wishing somehow that we were meant to be.

> But don't worry about me,

> Darkness caving in, but I think I'm supposed to learn to
> deal with it alone,

> And this time, maybe I'll save me on my own.

I see darkness in the corner of my room watching me.

        I see darkness in the corner of my room protecting me,

        Protecting me from the love I deserve.

        I see darkness in the corner of my room lurking,

        Growing,

        Waiting for me,

        Waiting for me to be happy

        So, it can take it away from me.

        Oh darkness, so kind,

        It shields me from happiness,

        It stops me from being at peace,

        It stops me from being me.

        So now when I see darkness,

        I see you.

~unorthodox ~

You're my long summer highs,
You're my lonely nights,

You're my 2am drives,

You're my 1st morning thoughts,

You're my blue skies,

You're my 2021,

And I could be the one,

If you let me

Not my words

But hers

Once hers, now mine to you

You're my grey skies and brown eyes,

You're my favourite takeaway,

You're my lifetime repeat song,

The one you never get tired of listening to

You weren't my everything,

Nor my first love,

But you were a close second,

and that's why I wish we never ended.

Soon you'll forget me,

And I'll be just another faded memory,

But

Don't hold on too tight,

Because

You might

Trip

And

Fall

Over

Our broken promises.

~Untitled~

I'm trying my best to get over you,
Because your skies make my heart so blue.
Not entirely sure if it all means pain,
Or if I'm going insane.
But why can't you see me?
It's like I'm here but we can't be,
I'm broken
Empty
Maybe I am losing my sanity.
My feelings for you- a burden I wish you could feel too.
The problem is that I wish not to be with yo,u
but I wish that you'd want to
It doesn't make sense I know,
But I don't know if I want to let go.
Because hurt is the only emotion that makes sense these
days
but I'm still hoping this is all a phase.
A momentary lapse of insanity,
Or perhaps a momentary lapse of honesty
Because I'm trying my best to get over you
But I also wish I didn't have to.

ReAlity

I don't believe in soulmates, but I can't help but feel
you've already found yours...

and left me behind,
I got left behind.

~ the way life goes.

CHAPTER FIVE

THE LESSONS

It's not about finding someone to save you,
It's about saving yourself because no one else will.

~CCA

We have reached the beginning of my journey.

I'm glad you are still here with me.

This chapter isn't about being upset about your past; it's

about using what you've experienced to better your

future. It's about the lessons I've learnt on the way here.

To my new beginning.

This is your life,

take back control.

because it wasn't your fault you've been hurt, but it is

your responsibility to heal from it.

I pray that God guides you on your journey from this point

forward, just as He has brought me to you <3

Because this is the part, I find me,

And I hope you find you too :)

I think for the longest time I thought that the perfect
person was going to fall at my feet when I was ready,
That one day I'd get all I asked for in a person,
But no.
What I've come to find is that the perfect person doesn't
exist.
I know I'm young, but I've spent most of my years
waiting for them.
The reality is, the only person you should be waiting for
is yourself
Waiting to find yourself,
Waiting to heal yourself,
Waiting to be the perfect person for yourself.
Because no one is going to save you.
The perfect person isn't going to come and save you,
You should save you.
And I'm not going to lie, I've met some pretty amazing
people in this lifetime so far,
but no one is ever going to be everything you need or
want in a person,
All you can do is learn to appreciate the tiny perfections
within the very flawed people you come across.
I think I heard that last part in a movie or something.
But the point is, don't waste your time looking for them,
when you could be the perfect person for you.

*"Bringing up the past, you may lose an eye but
if you don't, you will lose both of them,
because those unaware of the past are
condemned to repeat it"*
- heart breaking high

Stop expecting people to react in the way you want them to,
Because truth is, nobody's going to be there for you,
At least not always in the way you want them to.

Life is just an accumulation of experience,

    And

    I think sometimes people are scared of finding something
real.

    They run away from situations that make them feel too
much,

    but ce la vie.

    The key is to know when it is worth it to try and when it
is time to let go.

Soon you will come to realise that they don't care.

> They don't care about your absence.
>
> They never have and perhaps they never will.
>
> But that's okay,
>
> because now you have you.

They don't love you

      the way they used to.

      But don't give up on happiness because of that,

      Your roots will come someday,

      And this time, maybe they'll stay.

      So let go of the people who want to let you go.

      ~the way life goes.

I'm not in love with you.

      You don't love the way I want to be loved,

      So, I'm no longer in love with you.

      ~ I wish it were that easy.

Going through the hardest part of my life right now

And nobody's around,

I think that's just it,

That is what you must understand,

That maybe no one ever will be.

At least not permanently

Stop trying so hard for people to love you, they are going to
leave you eventually.
Because the ones who are true and for you, will stay, and
the ones who aren't, will be led astray.

When are you going to realise people don't care the
        way you do?
        When are you going to realise, your love is too rare to be
        found in other people?
        When are you going to open your eyes to the way people
        feel about you?
        You are loved but nobody likes you,
        Understand that,
        And move on.
        Because darling if you don't,
        You will spend the rest of your life searching for clouds
        in desert skies.

        ~the way life goes.

~Mastering...

It's okay darling,

Sometimes people leave without warning because they

weren't supposed to stay.

You will hurt,

But you will heal.

Sometimes I just wish people would tell me

that they no longer want to stay,

Because I'd be fine with the leaving, if it came with a

notice.

I don't understand ,

what I did

to make 'em leave,

But I've learnt that

sometimes people disappear without a trace and it is not

your fault but it is all part of the journey,

They come and then they go.

...the arts of letting go~

Listen to me darling,

      it was never meant to last forever, it never does.

~You are simply...

And eventually
No matter how hard you try,
But eventually
You will turn into your worst enemy.
The person you hate so much,
The person that hurt you so much.
You can't help it because it's true,
Hurt people, hurt people too,

so heal.

...a product of your environment ~

~You are simply...

The people around you are who make or break you,
So, surround yourself with good energy,

Because the best people always took you places.

...a product of your environment ~

And finally darling, allow yourself the space to feel,
Find something you like doing and then turn that
darkness into art.
Your art will always be beautiful,
because you have always been beautiful.

~ when the mind is not okay, the body doesn't stay.
So, heal the mind to stay alive.
~CCA

Books by C.C.A

Handpicked Roses:

Volume I: THE DEPTHS OF MY OWN SANITY

Volume II: UNDER

Volume III: OXYGEN | finding ways to breathe again.

Note From Author:

Thank you so much for reading my first book.

I have so much more to share with you. As you have already figured out by now, this book is part of a collection series titled:

'Handpicked Roses'

As my little gift to you, to thank you for making it to the end of this book, I will give you a little exclusive chapter 1 preview of the next book in this series.

It isn't out yet so SSSHHH, it'll be our little secret.

Mini disclaimer, it does get dark, so stop at any point it gets too much.

Once again, thank you for staying with me on this journey:)

CCA

UNDER

CCA

CONTENTS

Hi												1

Chapter 1 DOES IT GET BETTER?						2

DISCLAIMER										17

Chapter 2 THE WILTING ROSE							20

Chapter 3 THE BURNING HOUSE						30

Chapter 4 FIVE HUNDRED AND TEN						50

Chapter 5 TO THE PEOPLE WHO ARE STILL HERE			80

Chapter 6 DEAR JULIO								96

Chapter 7 READ THIS AFTER I'M GONE					122

CCA

UNDER

HI

I often feel the need to disappear
Sometimes from the world and other times from the
people around me
So I bury myself
Deep
Where no one can find me.
Into the depths of my insanity
But this time it is not just a new depth I feel.
This time I lose all of me,
Completely.
So this book I call 'under'
Where my only way out
is to continue going down.

CHAPTER 1

DOES IT GET BETTER?

Maybe getting better was never part of my story,
but to every story, there is an ending, so perhaps we've reached the
end of mine.

Never felt so lonely in my entire life 'till this
point right here.
No one feels right anymore.
I don't want to burden another soul with my own
darkness.
Struggling,
Fighting,
Breaking again,
But this time
I don't understand why.

I wish I had some type of outlet or
     escape for my worries.
     But I don't.
     So I'm forced to live within the confines of my own
     being
     Hoping one day that this vessel would finally let me go,
     Finally set me free.

UNDER

Is it that
I'm so good at hiding my own pain
Or do they just not care enough to see
what is wrong with me?

Nightmares

Nightmares
Negative thoughts
What's the difference?
One torments you when you're asleep,
The other one torments you while you're awake.
Face reality
There is no escaping love,
Maybe death will help you
to find what you're looking for.
But once you have your meeting with her,
You can never return,
So choose wisely dear
Don't let go until you are ready.

UNDER

I need to stop hurting myself
But I'm not hungry
I can't eat anything.

The unremarkable person

My thoughts:
You don't matter.
Not a single soul in the world is made for you.
In a world where you will be broken a billion times
And your experience doesn't matter,
Learn to give up.
Where the people you love will leave you
And no one around you is there for you,
Learn to leave too.

My heart:
But even when the world turns its back on me,
And the people I love, set me free,
 I will continue to love.

UNDER

Last meal was Sunday,
　　　　But I ate today, today is Thursday.

But how do I get better now that I'm here,

At the bottom of the deep end?

Just keep swimming…

UNDER

Things often change quickly for me.
        Emotions
        Moods
        Feelings
        So I tend to hold things in
        In hopes that the rains of today don't wet the skies of
        tomorrow
        But each time
        I come to find
        The large puddles on the ground that linger the following
        days
        Each time, when the sun decides to shine and the
        darkness seems to fade,
        The clouds cry a little harder
        Each day, no better than the last
        And I learn all over again
        that the rain of yesterday
        Not only wets the skies of the next
        but leads way for a storm.

        Then I begin to drown
        All over again
        In the floods of yesterday and the puddles of tomorrow.

I was made of rain clouds 24.02.22

Is it all my fault
Why things never seem to work out?
How do I tell them?
That I'm ready to give up
How do I tell them?
This hole I'm falling in
Just seems to get deeper the more I try to climb out of it
Nothing seems to be working
And I've been trying for so long
I think it's time
To let go
Will the skies ever stop raining?
Will I ever be
Nicer,
Better,
Enough?

UNDER

I don't understand
       why I'm still here.
       I've tried so many times
       To give up
       To let go
       But I keep coming back here
       To the same point
       Reliving the same thoughts
       Moments
       All over again
       And I don't understand why
       Who I hurt
       What I did
       To lead me to this point
       Why do I have to keep living, breathing, being
       When it's not even in the way I want to?
       Why can't I let go?
       Why can't I be set free?

You know when you sleep relatively okay,
>and then you wake up and lose the motivation to exist?
>Yeah,
>That's how I feel today.

UNDER

Water doesn't even feel like water anymore
When I shower or bathe
I don't feel clean
I just want to keep on scrubbing
until every part of me is gone.

I wish I could close my eyes forever,
> And never have to wake from this blissful slumber.

The Fallen Angel

I feel like life keeps hitting me with things that will eventually kill
me
Perhaps that is what I desire,
For a fire
That will devour all that I am,
So when I say I couldn't escape
No one will blame me.
Maybe I want my world to come crashing down
Like billions of falling rocks
So that they trample me in my attempt to flee
And the birds in the sky will look down and wonder how a human
being could be so unlucky.
And in a world where God is good, where does He stand in it all?
At the end or in between?
Has He finally given up on me?
I once heard that
life gets tough when you're the closest to getting what you want
But what if all I want for my final destination
Is to just not be here anymore?
Who then gains the next score?
God, or the fallen angel?
Tell me once more,
How I should keep trying for a life I do not fully wish to live
Tell me again,
how I should keep going on for a life where all I have to give
isn't enough to save me?
And then at what point do I start living for me?

Printed in Great Britain
by Amazon